A self-guided walk through Green-Wood Cemetery

WALK #1: BATTLE HILL AND BACK

Written by Jeffrey I. Richman

A self-guided
Green-Wood

walk through Cemetery

featuring:

BROOKLYN THEATRE FIRE
F.A.O. SCHWARZ
SOLDIERS' MONUMENT
LEONARD BERNSTEIN
CHARLES EBBETTS
ELIAS HOWE
MARCUS DALY
ELMER SPERRY
JOHNNY TORRIO
HENRY CHADWICK
CHARLOTTE CANDA
JANE GRIFFITH
DE WITT CLINTON
NATHANIEL CURRIER
. . . and many more

Welcome . . .

On behalf of the Board of Trustees, I would like to welcome you to The Green-Wood Cemetery.

Founded in 1838 as the third rural cemetery in America, Green-Wood has become one of the great cemeteries of the world. We are proud to share this historic place with you.

A century and one-half ago, Green-Wood Cemetery was one of 19th century America's leading tourist attractions. By the 1850's, 500,000 people were passing through our gates every year, walking its paths and riding through it on carriage tours. We would like to renew that tradition of public access and enjoyment.

Green-Wood Cemetery has a great deal to offer. It is a remarkable arboretum, wildlife sanctuary, sculpture garden, a place of architecture, landscape design, and history. This tour will give you a chance to enjoy all of these aspects of the cemetery.

This is the first of a planned series of walking guides. It will get you out into the cemetery, allow you to take in its unique grounds, and lead you back out. Please enjoy yourself while you are here as our guest. Also, please keep in mind that this is an active cemetery, with an average of five funerals per day and a steady stream of families visiting their loved ones. We ask you to respect them at all times.

The cemetery is open to visitors everyday from 8:00 a.m. to 4:00 p.m., weather permitting. Enjoy the cemetery and stop by our offices if you have any questions or comments.

Richard J. Moylan
President
The Green-Wood Cemetery

To Battle Hill and Back

This tour begins inside the cemetery, at its brownstone main gates, about 100 yards east of the intersection of 25th Street and Fifth Avenue. The tour covers 1.4 miles, and some of the walking is up and down hills.

The approximate time to walk this tour is two to three hours; it has been divided into two sections so that you can, if you prefer, do the first part of the tour (covering approximately 1 mile) on one day, then the second part (.4 of a mile) some other time.

For the purposes of this walk, it will be assumed that the cemetery runs squarely east/west and north/south. Therefore, as you walk through the cemetery's brownstone gates, east is straight ahead, west directly behind you, north to your left, and south to your right.

Also note that distances in feet are often given in the tour directions. You are not expected to carry a tape measure as you walk. Rather, those distances should give you an idea of distance; you can approximate the length of your stride at 3 feet.

This photograph, circa 1860, shows the stone yards which clustered near Green-Wood Cemetery's main entrance at Fifth Avenue and 25th Street.

Begin the tour at the cemetery's brownstone main gates, about 100 yards east of the intersection of 25th Street and Fifth Avenue.

Before you head farther into the cemetery, look west, back toward Fifth Avenue, where you entered the cemetery. During the 19th century, the intersections at the entrances to Green-Wood Cemetery were lined with monument makers and flower shops catering to cemetery visitors.

On the southwest corner of this intersection stands the McGovern-Weir Greenhouse. It has been serving visitors to Green-Wood since it was built in 1895, and is the only Victorian commercial greenhouse still standing in New York City.

The landmarked brownstone cemetery gates which rise above you were built by Richard Upjohn and Son from 1861 to 1863. In Gothic Revival style, they rise 106 feet, pointing toward heaven. The yellow sandstone reliefs, by English-born sculptor John Moffitt, reflect the cemetery's resurrectionist attitude: they are *Come Forth, The Dead Shall Be Raised, I Am the Resurrection and the Life,* and *Weep Not.*

Take a moment to listen; you may hear the noisy monk parrots which have made their home near the top of the gate towers. The founders of this parrot colony were natives of Argentina who escaped years ago from a shipment going through Kennedy Airport. The birds are predominantly green with some blue, yellow, and gray.

Before you begin your trip farther into the cemetery, you may want to stop off at the public restroom which is just inside the main gates, to your left. This is the only restroom you will pass on this tour.

Walk through the left entrance of the brownstone gates and go about 50 feet until you reach the road which heads off to the left (north). Stop there. This is **STOP #1**.

Look down this road and note the flat area of graves to its right, in front of the wooden fence in the distance. This is the Meadow, an area of the cemetery occupied in the 19th century by housing for cemetery employees, and which was devoted to burials in the early 1970's. Because this area is relatively recently developed, and many of the deceaseds' families and friends are frequent visitors there, it is often colorfully decorated with holiday wreaths and flowers.

As you stand at this intersection, note the monuments along the right side of this road, about 15 feet northeast of the intersection. Until recently, there were very few photographs in the cemetery; this practice of memorializing the dead with photographs of them in life is common in other areas of the world, and has become very popular for recent burials at Green-Wood Cemetery.

Standing at this intersection, one road heads to the left (north), one goes straight ahead up the hill (east), and the other proceeds to the right (south). Start up the middle road (Battle Avenue), heading east up the hill.

Note the row of low trees along the left side of Battle Avenue. All of these (except the third tree up, which is a camperdown elm grafted to a scotch elm) are weeping mulberry trees. Not surprisingly, weeping trees, particularly weeping willows (which prefer moist soil and can be found near Green-Wood Cemetery's ponds), are very popular in cemetery's for their symbolic relationship to mourning.

Proceed up Battle Avenue to the first intersection, where Arbor Avenue comes down from the right. On the southwest corner of this intersection (on your right as you approach it) is the Stewart Mausoleum. This is **STOP #2**.

Here lie the parents of Isabella Stewart Gardner; the famous art museum that she established, and which bears her name, is in Boston. **David Stewart** (1810–1891) made his

The Stewart Tomb is decorated with resurrectionist bronzes by Stanford White and Augustus Saint-Gaudens.

money in coal and steel. He hired the great artists, designer Stanford White and sculptor Augustus Saint-Gaudens, to decorate this tomb. Their bronze reliefs, dating from 1883, feature robed angels. At the time they were installed they were controversial because of their depiction of death as something other than gloomy. These bronzes were cleaned and restored in 1998.

Stand with your back to the Stewart Mausoleum. Just over 100 feet straight in front of you, across Battle Avenue, you will see a dark granite monument topped by a cross with the round bronze seal of the A.S.P.C.A. on its front and "Louis Bonard" printed across its bottom. Walk over to it. This is **STOP #3**.

Here lies **Louis Bonard** (1809–1871), a French immigrant who made money in real estate investments and from his inventions. In 1871, on his deathbed, Bonard summoned Henry Bergh, the founder of the American Society for the Prevention of Cruelty to Animals, to his hovel, a tiny apartment on Mulberry Street, and offered Bergh his fortune. That fortune, in a trunk at the foot of his bed, totaled what

would be about $1.8 million in today's money. The A.S.P.C.A., in thanks, placed this monument to Bonard. Note the tribute to him on its right side: "MUTE ANIMALS SHARE HIS COMPASSIONATE BOUNTY."

Follow the path which is just in front of the Bonard Monument, and runs along Battle Avenue, up the hill to the next intersection, where Bay View Avenue comes in from the left. Directly in front of you, at the northeast corner of this intersection, is a large gray obelisk, the Brooklyn Theatre Fire Monument. This is **STOP #4**.

The monument to Louis Bonard bears the A.S.P.C.A.'s seal on its front.

Flames consume the Brooklyn Theatre in this contemporary woodcut.

On December 5, 1876, the Brooklyn Theatre, in downtown Brooklyn, was packed with 1,000 patrons enjoying a very popular play of the time, *The Two Orphans*. As the actors on stage moved the play towards its final minutes, they heard "fire" whispered from the wings, then saw flames rising there. The stagehands tried to control the fire, but were unable to do so, and it spread. Though the actors came to the front of the stage and tried to calm the audience, a panic ensued, and within half an hour the building collapsed.

It was at first thought that there had been little loss of life, but the next day, as firemen picked through the rubble, they recovered 278 bodies.

Within days, a mass burial of 103 of the victims, whose bodies had not been claimed or whose families could not afford a burial, were interred in a mass grave around this monument. Walk up to the monument and read the inscriptions on its sides.

This contemporary woodcut shows the unclaimed victims of the Brooklyn Theatre Fire being placed in a common grave at Green-Wood Cemetery.

The Brooklyn Theatre Fire Monument, in a photograph circa 1890. The fence is no longer there.

Proceed north on Bay View Avenue, continuing approximately 60 feet past Bay View Path, to the white marble monument to **Louis Moreau Gottschalk** (1829–1869) which appears on your right. This is **STOP #5**.

Gottschalk was born in New Orleans to a German-Jewish father and a Creole mother who was an accomplished singer. At an early age he showed musical ability, and went off to Europe to study the piano. But when he applied for admission to the Paris Conservatory, he was rejected without an audition, the director of classes explaining that his school was no place for someone from America, "the country of railroads but not of musicians."

Gottschalk managed to find a teacher in Paris, was befriended by Hector Berlioz, and toured Europe to acclaim. At the age of sixteen he played for Chopin, who was duly impressed, predicting Gottschalk would "become the king of pianists." In 1853, Gottschalk made his American debut at Niblo's in New York City, then toured the United States, Mexico, and South America. He was the first important American composer, was the first American musician with a national and international reputation, was the first from his country to popularize concert music, and was a brilliant pianist who shone playing his own very difficult compositions. Gottschalk's music combined Creole, black, minstrel, South American, Spanish, mariachi, West Indian, and Cuban sounds.

Matinee idol Louis Moreau Gottschalk.

Though music critics were divided on Gottschalk's talents, his popularity in America was enormous, rivaled only by that of Jenny Lind, the Swedish Nightingale. At his concerts, he always wore white gloves which he dramatically removed on stage one finger at a time. Female admirers would then storm on stage, tearing the gloves to pieces as they fought for souvenirs. A showman and a Don Juan, Gottschalk was fluent in five languages. Gottschalk, who never married, was run out of San Francisco for his romantic escapades, and was threatened by men throughout the country who believed that he had used his good looks and matinee-idol status to corrupt the morals of their wives.

A committed Unionist and abolitionist, Gottschalk toured Civil War battlefields, playing for the troops. On November 24, 1869, while leading 600 musicians in a performance of his own composition *Morte!! (She is Dead)*, he fell ill, and succumbed a month later.

This 19th century photograph shows Gottschalk's white marble monument topped by an angel holding an open book on which appeared the titles of six of his most famous compositions.

Retrace your steps back south along Bay View Avenue to the intersection with Battle Avenue; turn left and continue across the intersection to the southeast corner. This is **STOP #6**.

This wonderful cluster of sculpture is all anonymous. Included here is the monument to **Henry Aaron Burr** (1811–1884), a relative of Vice President Aaron Burr's. Henry Aaron Burr made his fortune from a hat-forming machine he invented; during the 1850's, 6 million of his machines were in use in America. Burr was also the long-time president of the board of trustees of New York City's Volunteer Fire Department. At the outbreak of the Civil War, Burr helped organize and finance Elmer Ellsworth's red-coated Fire Zoaves, one of the most famous regiments of the war.

Walk up the stairs to the Burr monument, take a closer look at the fine sculpture around it, then continue straight back from the Burr monument 45 feet to the monument to Alice and Phoebe Cary ("CARY" is across the base). This is **STOP #7**.

Alice and Phoebe Cary.

Sisters **Alice Cary** (1820–1871) and **Phoebe Cary** (1824–1871) led "the Cary Salon," a cultural circle which met every Sunday evening at their 20th Street home in Manhattan. Regulars at their "trysting place of Liberty" were women's rights advocates Susan B. Anthony and Elizabeth Cady Stanton, writer Fanny Fern, reformer Horace Greeley, newspaperman Robert Bonner, poet John Greenleaf Whittier, and showman P.T. Barnum. Barnum considered Phoebe to be "the wittiest woman in America."

Note the dates of death engraved on this granite stone. Alice was ill for many years, and Phoebe nursed her, forsaking marriage, until her death in 1871. Within five months of Alice's death, Phoebe, who until the death of her beloved sister had been in good health, was buried beside her.

With your back to the front of the Cary monument, look north across Battle Avenue. About 20 feet beyond the road in the first row of monuments, you will see a circular bronze relief, set in granite, of William Wheatley (his name is on the

left hand side of the monument, as you face it). Walk over there, taking the stairs, which are on a straight line with the Wheatley monument, down to the road. This is **STOP #8**.

One of the original Black Crook *showgirls, showing off her tights.*

William Wheatley (1816–1876), actor, theatre manager, and producer, is best known today for his role as the producer of the *Black Crook*, the first modern American musical. That show, which opened in 1866, was a spectacular in four acts which ran for five and one-half hours. It featured 300 babies crawling across the stage and scores of singers, dancers, and musicians. But its greatest attraction was its showgirls, who appeared on stage in flesh-colored tights, a scandalous display for the time, and drove the predominately-male audience wild with lively renditions of such catchy tunes as *You Naughty, Naughty Men*.

Follow Battle Avenue east up the hill to the next intersection, where Highland Avenue comes in from the right. On the southwest corner of this intersection stands the Roach family plot, which has at its center a large granite stone topped by a female figure and "JOHN ROACH" across its base. This is **STOP #9**.

John Roach (1815–1887) came to America as a penniless Irish immigrant and became its foremost marine engine manufacturer and shipbuilder. He was the leader of the American iron hull shipping industry and built the first steel warships for the United States Navy. For many years this plot was surrounded by a fence; now only the stone entranceway still stands.

Continue up the hill to the east side of this intersection of Battle Avenue and Highland Avenue. Walk up the long stairs to the Anderson Tomb ("JOHN ANDERSON" is spelled near its top), which stands atop the hill overlooking the intersection. This is **STOP #10**.

John Anderson (1812–1881) was a prominent New Yorker who found fame and fortune as a tobacconist. In 1842, he was talked about as a possible candidate for New York City mayor, but when he came under suspicion for the death of Mary Cecilia Rogers, the "Beautiful Seegar Girl" who had worked in his store, his political ambitions were dashed.

This engraving shows Mary Rogers's body floating in the Hudson River.

Anderson is interred in this Greek Revival temple, built in the 1860's as a statement of his commitment to democratic ideals, including his support for Italian unification and the Union. Note the four statuettes decorating the tomb; they are signed by John Moffitt, the sculptor who is responsible for several other works at the cemetery. Stand on the steps of the Anderson tomb and look back toward Green-Wood's main gates; enjoy the spectacular view of New York harbor and the skyline.

Walk around the right side of the Anderson Tomb and behind it, then go 85 feet past it and slightly to the right toward

This was the view from John Anderson's tomb, circa 1890, with Green-Wood Cemetery's main gates to the left, and New York's ship-filled harbor in the distance.

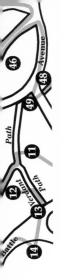

F.A.O. Schwarz's grave at Green-Wood Cemetery.

F.A.O. Schwarz's toy store has grown into a national chain. This sign is outside its Fifth Avenue store.

a row of six identical gray granite stones, about 3 feet high, with slightly pointed tops. This is **STOP #11**.

In this group is the stone memorializing **Frederick Augustus Otto Schwarz** (1836–1911), the German immigrant who came to New York City in 1870 and founded Schwarz's Toy Bazaar on Broadway. FAO Schwarz has grown into a world famous toy store chain with close to forty branches across America.

Stand in front of F.A.O. Schwarz's monument and look over it; you will see Verdant Path and Greenbank Path intersecting. Walk east to that intersection, then continue in the same direction along Greenbank Path. As you do so, note the variety of architectural styles in the hillside mausoleums. When you reach the Wallace Mausoleum, which will be the third mausoleum on your right, about 75 feet from the intersection of the paths, stop and look to your left; there is a large granite monument, topped by a cross. Walk to the front of that monument to admire the marble bust of actor **Barney Williams** (1823–1876). This is **STOP #12**.

Born Bernard Flaherty in Cork, Ireland, he came to this country as a boy with his family; his father became a grocer, then a boarding-house keeper near the Bowery in New York. Bernard adopted "Barney Williams" as his name when he took to the stage. He soon found his place in New York theater playing good-natured Irish roles, and was known for his character, "Ragged Pat." In 1850, he married popular actress/singer Maria Pray, and they played together thereafter as co-stars. Often he appeared in the role of the hard-drinking lovable Irishman, and she as a pert Yankee woman. His acting was well-received in the United States, Canada, and Great Britain, and upon his death he left a large fortune. The day after his death the *New York Tribune* editorialized that his acting career had been "a very important work in his little world" and lauded him for the good cheer he had always brought to his audiences. "Irish Barney," with his blue eyes twinkling and his rich brogue, was, as one commentator said, "a capital and infectiously humorous entertainer, in broad and Irish character, and as such greatly loved and amply rewarded by the public."

Return to Verdant Path, then follow it to the right. As you reach Battle Avenue, note the hitching post where Verdant Path meets the road. This is **STOP #13**.

These handsome pieces, which are scattered through the cemetery, date from the 19th century, and were used by visitors during the horse and buggy era to tie their horses up and prevent them from wandering away.

Now proceed to the right (from Verdant Path), up Battle Avenue about 75 feet to its intersection with Bay View Avenue (which comes in from the left).

Examples of an early cast iron hitching post and a path sign at Green-Wood Cemetery. Over the years, some of these signs have deteriorated and been replaced with new stamped signs. Green-Wood Cemetery has recently made arrangements to cast replacement signs in the old design.

Note the wonderful cast iron sign for Bay View Avenue, one of many such early pieces which have survived a century and one-half outdoors.

Just 20 feet behind the Bay View Avenue sign stands the Van Ness-Parsons Pyramid. Walk up to the front; this is **STOP #14**.

Though this tomb appears to be ancient, it probably dates from the 1920's or 1930's. **Albert Parsons** (1847–1933),

Detail of the entrance to the Van Ness-Parsons tomb.

who is interred inside it, was an Egyptologist whose book, *The New Light From the Pyramids*, attracted international attention. Note the fascinating mix in front of the tomb, as well as on its door, of Christian and Egyptian images and figures. Above the doorway is the symbol of Osiris, the Egyptian god responsible for protecting temples.

Continue up Battle Avenue 225 feet, passing Green-Bank Path, until you reach two sets of stairs about 20 feet apart; walk up the second set of stairs, which has "16488" carved at its top. Nearly 30 feet beyond the top of the stairs is a gray granite tree trunk. Walk up to it. This is **STOP #15**.

This simple monument to **Alfred Van Derwerken, Jr.** (1870–1906) is symbolically similar to the cut-off column often seen in the cemetery; both symbolize a young man whose life was cut-off before it reached its full height. This unusual tree stump is a very special monument dedicated to a man who "loved nature."

The monument to Alfred Van Derwerken, Jr.

Return down the steps to Battle Avenue. Turn right on Battle Avenue and continue up the hill. At the next intersection, where Border Avenue comes in from the left, you will see a long stairway on the northeast corner, going up the hill; proceed up it onto Battle Hill stopping at the top of the stairs. This is **STOP #16**.

Green-Wood Cemetery's Soldiers' Monument commemorates the New Yorkers who served during the Civil War. This photograph, circa 1870, shows three of the soldiers holding their accouterments.

At the top of this stairway stands the Soldiers' Monument. Erected in 1869, it honors the 148,000 New York men who fought for the Union during the Civil War. It was built only four years after the Civil War, very early for such a monument; most Civil War monuments date from the 1880's and 1890's. The four soldiers here represent four different branches of service; originally, one soldier held an ax, another a rifle, the third a rammer, and the last a sword.

As you stand at the top of the stairway, with the Soldiers' Monument in front of you, Battle Path goes to the left. Head to the left (north) about 60 feet on Battle Path to where it forks; follow the left fork just a few feet until you reach a small gray rectangular stone, at ground level, about 4 feet to the right of the edge of the path, with "TILTON" on it. This is **STOP #17**.

In the same plot, on its right side as you face it from the path, and just next to the path that circles the Soldiers' Monument, is a slightly raised stone on which appears, "GRANDMOTHER."

"Grandmother" in this plot is **Elizabeth Tilton** (1834–1897), whose affair with the "Great Divine," the Rev. Henry Ward Beecher, one of the moral leaders of 19th century America, shook America. Beecher was the long-time leader

Henry Beecher, Elizabeth Tilton, and Theodore Tilton, the principal players in "The Great Scandal."

of Plymouth Church in Brooklyn Heights and Elizabeth Tilton was a schoolmate of one of Beecher's daughters and was active in the church. She was married to Theodore Tilton (Beecher presided at their wedding), who was a close friend of Beecher's.

Henry Ward Beecher (1813–1887) and Elizabeth Tilton had an affair in 1868, and court and church proceedings resulting from it culminated in the "Trial of the Century" in 1876. That six-month trial, in which Beecher insisted that he could not have had an affair with Elizabeth Tilton because he was too moral a person, ended with the jury hung 9-3 in favor of Beecher.

As a result of this scandal, the Tilton family was torn apart. Theodore Tilton left the United States in 1883 and spent the rest of his life living in Paris. Elizabeth Tilton, ostracized by everyone except her daughter and a radical group known as the "Christian Friends," died lonely and blind in 1897.

Note that this plot, a prime spot in the cemetery, has no central monument. This is a result of the impact of this scandal on the Tilton family. Henry Ward Beecher is buried, with his wife, on a Green-Wood Cemetery hillside about one-half mile to the east.

Proceed further (north) along Battle Path to the large bronze statue of Minerva. This is **STOP #18**.

This is *Minerva and the Altar of Liberty*. It was the long-time ambition of Charles Higgins, who made his fortune with "Higgins' American India Ink" at his Ninth Street factory in Brooklyn, to appropriately commemorate the Battle of Long Island, the first Revolutionary War battle fought by American forces after the Declaration of Independence.

The crowd gathers for the 1920 dedication of Minerva and the Altar of Liberty.

Note Higgins's tomb, which stands just behind *Minerva*.

Minerva, the goddess of battle and protector of civilized life, salutes her sister, the Statue of Liberty, in the harbor. Stand just behind Minerva and look through the trees to enjoy the spectacular view of New York harbor.

Battle Hill in Green-Wood Cemetery is named for the Battle of Long Island. The first known interments on this land, which occurred 62 years before the cemetery was founded, were of American soldiers who buried where they fell during this battle in 1776.

Walk back (south) a few feet on Battle Path and turn left onto Liberty Path. Proceed east 100 feet on Liberty Path; on your right, between two rows of ivy, and across Liberty Path from a large granite obelisk, is the Bernstein plot. A stone bench marked "BERNSTEIN" is at the back of the plot, between two large evergreen shrubs. This is **STOP #19**.

For nearly half of the 20th century, **Leonard Bernstein** (1918–1990) was a leading figure in the music world. He excelled as a conductor, composer of classical music and Broadway shows, pianist, and music teacher. His wife, **Felice Montelegre**, is buried beside him.

There may be some small stones on his gravestone. It is a Jewish tradition to leave a stone at graveside as a token of remembrance.

Proceed 50 feet farther (east) down Liberty Path, then turn to the left into the Litchfield plot ("LITCHFIELD" is carved on the steps) which is surrounded by a stone enclosure. This is **STOP #20**.

It is a Jewish tradition, dating back centuries, to leave a small stone at graveside as a token of a visit to pay respects to the deceased. The accompanying photograph, taken shortly after Bernstein's death, shows several such stones. The one with a paper strip across it is marked "Vienna Philharmonic," an orchestra which Bernstein often led.

In the grove of trees in front of you, **Edward Litchfield** (1815–1885) is buried. Litchfield was a leading Brooklyn real estate developer and was the force behind Park Slope's growth. Litchfield lived in the building that is now the headquarters for the Parks Department in Prospect Park. Returning from a trip abroad in the mid-19th century, Litchfield learned that the land around his home had been taken by the City of Brooklyn for inclusion in Prospect Park. It is said that Litchfield, in protest, insisted that he be buried facing away from Prospect Park.

As you come out of the Litchfield plot, turn right and follow Liberty Path (west) back 25 feet just past the Farhood stone, which is on your right. Turn right off the path and walk north, next to the Litchfield stone fence, toward the hill in front of you. That hill is topped by the tomb of Philip and Latifee Kiamie (their names are carved across its top). Continue in the direction of the hill and the Kiamie tomb until you reach the road which crosses in front of you, Garland Avenue. Now, look back south, in the direction you have just come from; you should see the long monument to Alonzo B. See. It has benches to both sides of a female figure; "Alonzo B. See" appears to the left and below the central female figure. This is **STOP #21**.

Alonzo B. See (1849–1941) was an obscure elevator manufacturer until 1922, when he became "suddenly famous" by replying to a request from Adelphi College for funds to educate young women with the statement that "all women's colleges should be burned." His pronouncement sparked a national controversy and caused many readers of *The New York Times* to "hit the ceiling faster than they ever ascended in one of the See elevators."

Perhaps in apology for his sin, Alonzo B. See's monument features this idealized female figure.

Turn around on Garland Avenue so that you now have your back to Alonzo B. See's monument and are facing north toward the hillside.

You are looking at the highest point in Brooklyn. The gravestones on this hillside are from the 20th century; this hill, for many years, was topped by a reservoir. About two-thirds

Beloved Ebbets Field, 1913–1960. Rest in peace.

23

of the way up the hill, and slightly to the left of the Kiamie tomb which tops it, is the grave of **Charles H. Ebbets** (1859–1925), who made the Brooklyn Dodgers and Ebbets Field Brooklyn institutions. His family plot is marked by a large, light-colored stone with "EBBETS" carved across it. It's worth a trip up the hillside to pay your respects to Charles Ebbets, to enjoy the view from the top, and to be able to tell your friends that you stood on the highest point in Brooklyn.

Returning to Garland Avenue, go east (to your left as you come down the hill, to your right as you face the hillside) on it until you reach Canna Path; turn left onto it and walk approximately 60 paces. There, to your left, you will see the gray granite monument to civil engineer **Ole Singstad** (1882–1969). This is **STOP #22**.

These gravestones memorialize Charles Ebbets, Sr., who died on April 18, 1925. His funeral was held a week later, on a cold and rainy day, and new Dodger Club President Ed McKeever caught the flu and died four days later. On the day of Ebbets's funeral, all National League baseball games were cancelled.

He was the designer or consultant on an entire generation of motor vehicle tunnels, including the Holland, Lincoln, Queens Midtown, Brooklyn-Battery tunnels, and twin rapid transit tubes under the East River in New York City, the Baltimore Harbor Tunnel, the Hudson Tubes from New Jersey to Manhattan, the tube between Oakland and Alameda, California, the Callahan and Sumner tunnels in Boston, and the West Virginia Memorial Tunnel at Wheeling.

Singstad felt that his greatest accomplishment was the three-tiered ventilation system which he designed for the Holland Tunnel. When it opened, it was the first underwater automobile highway in the world. On November 12, 1927, at

4:00 p.m., President Calvin Coolidge, aboard the Presidential yacht, pushed a button that rang a brass bell at the tunnel's entrance to signal its opening. Officials, however, wary of disaster, held up all traffic until midnight in the hopes that the fewer cars at that hour would limit the strain on the tunnel. Singstad recalled the opening day:

> I couldn't wait to enjoy my tunnel and so when the speeches were over, I set out to walk through it alone. Soon I heard a rumbling, shuffling sound in the distance. "Good God!" I thought, "it sounds like an ocean, like the tunnel's caved in!" I jumped up to the elevated sidewalk. My fears were happily unfounded. The noise came from hundreds of people who, prevented from driving through the tunnel, had parked their cars and were walking — some pushing baby carriages — through what I don't mind calling a new wonder of the world.

Late in his life, Singstad regretted that so many of the tunnels that he helped to build were for cars and so few were for mass transit.

Continue along Canna Path another 20 paces; on your left you will see the monument to **William F. Mangels** (1866–1958). This is **STOP #23**.

Working in Coney Island, Mangels played a key role in the creation of the great American amusement parks at the turn of the century. He was one of the leading manufacturers of carousels in America. He invented the Whip ride, and designed the wave pool at Palisades Amusement Park in New Jersey. Other rides that he invented were copied throughout the world. But it was Mangels's Tickler that prompted P.G. Wodehouse, apparently as he fought nausea and bruises, to pick up his pen and write:

> The principle at the bottom of Coney Island's success is the eminently sound one that what would be a brutal assault, if administered gratis, becomes a rollicking pleasure when charged for at the rate of fifteen cents per assault. Suppose one laid hand upon you and put you in a large tub; suppose he then proceeded to send the tub spinning down an incline so arranged that at intervals of a few feet it spun around and violently bumped into something. Next day he would hear from your lawyer. But in Coney Island you jump into the Tickler and enjoy it; you have to enjoy it because you have paid good money to do so. Being in America, Coney Island is

thought a little vulgar; if it were in France we would have written how essentially refined the Tickler and the Human Roulette Wheel were, and with what abundance and polish the French people took its pleasure.

The Tickler, one of William Mangels's inspirations, was forty seconds in a tub as it twirled on casters down an incline. One oberserver described the ride as to "be packed in a monster barrel and be rolled incontinently down a hill. . . . There are milder things than that barrel shown in European museums in execration of the Spanish Inquisition."

Continue another few paces along Canna Path to the intersection of the paths; there make a right turn and follow the path to Hemlock Avenue. Turn left on Hemlock Avenue and walk 35 paces; on the left side of the road you will see a tomb, topped by an angel, with "JOHN TORRIO" across the front. This is **STOP #24**.

Johnny Torrio (1882–1957) was Al Capone's boss and the brains behind the Chicago Syndicate. He retired to Brooklyn in 1925, lived off his fortune, and acted as a Mob elder statesman.

Turning your back to the Torrio tomb, walk across Hemlock Avenue to the opposite (southeast) corner, where Hemlock intersects Border Avenue. This is **STOP #25**.

There, in the Koch family plot, an idealized woman holds a bronze plaque with the portrait of **Clara Ruppertz Koch** (1861–1919), "THE BEST WOMAN THAT EVER LIVED."

From this corner, go diagonally to the right across Border Avenue and look between two large monuments, one with "OHLANDT" carved across it, the other marked "RICKE." Between and behind them is the splendid Chadwick monument, topped by an oversized gray granite baseball, about 36 feet off the road. This is **STOP #26**.

No man did more to make baseball the American pastime than **Henry Chadwick** (1824–1908). He was America's first baseball editor, created the baseball scoring system in which numbers were assigned to each position (as in a 6 to 4 to 3 double play), introduced the newspaper box score, and coined some of baseball's most-enduring phrases, including "assist," "base hit," "base on balls," "cut off," "chin music," "fungo," "white wash," "double play," "error," "goose egg," "left on base," and "single." Chadwick also edited yearly baseball guides and was in charge of changes in baseball rules. President Theodore Roosevelt dubbed him the "Father of Baseball" and he is a member of the Baseball Hall of Fame in Cooperstown, N.Y.

This monument, topped by a granite baseball, has wonderful bronze pieces on it, including a glove, crossed bats, and a catcher's mask. Appropriately, the plaque on the front of the monument, which memorializes Chadwick, is in the shape of a baseball diamond. This monument was placed at Green-Wood by a committee chaired by Charles Ebbets, whose grave is nearby.

Note the granite bases that mark the four corners of the Chadwick plot.

The remarkable monument to the "Father of Baseball." For years, Charles Ebbets, owner of the Brooklyn Dodgers, led an annual pilgrimage of baseball's faithful to Chadwick's grave, where they laid a wreath in his honor. Appropriately, Ebbets is buried on a nearby hillside.

Retrace your route back to the intersection that you just came from, where Hemlock Avenue and Border Avenue meet, then turn left and head back south along Hemlock Avenue. After you pass Canna Path, note the long, low Sperry Monument on your right. This is **STOP #27**.

In front of the Sperry family memorial, at ground level, is the memorial to **Elmer Ambrose Sperry** (1860–1930), one of the most prolific and important inventors of the 20th

century. His greatest invention was the gyroscope, which revolutionized navigation. He founded what later became the Sperry-Rand Corporation.

Continue south on Hemlock Avenue another 60 feet. Just before you get to the Seamans Tomb along the right side of the road, look to the right about 90 feet and you will see a monument carved "TRIPPE." This is **STOP #28**.

This is the plot where **Juan Terry Trippe** (1899–1981), the founder of Pan American Airways who built it into a billion dollar international power, is buried.

Proceed south on Hemlock Avenue to the intersection with Garland Avenue. On the southeast corner, towering above and to the right of the large tomb marked "M. HERMANN," are two ginkgo trees. This is **STOP #29**.

The ginkgo is one of the oldest plants on earth, dating back 150 million years. These trees were thought to have become extinct until they were found in a remote area of China during the 20th century. Some ginkgo trees produce a foul smelling yellow-orange fleshy covered seed; it is impossible to tell until the tree matures whether it will produce these. If you're in an adventurous mood, check under the tree for these seeds.

As you walk along the second block, between Garland Avenue and Battle Avenue, note the three large chestnut trees along the left side. This is **STOP #30**. You should see many chestnuts on the ground below them.

Turn left onto Battle Avenue and proceed two-thirds of the way down the block, until you reach Lake Path; stop there. This is **STOP #31**.

Standing at Lake Path, look farther down Battle Avenue to the hillside ahead. Notice that the gravestones there are less elaborate than the monuments around you. That hillside is one of the public lots in the cemetery, where gravesites could be purchased in the 19th century for a few dollars. You may notice some brownstone gravestones on this hillside; they predate Green-Wood Cemetery, and were moved here from old church burial grounds.

Turn right onto Lake Path and walk 30 feet; on your right you will see the monument to William Kingsley with a bronze plaque across its front. This is **STOP #32**.

William Kingsley (1833–1885) was the general contractor for the Brooklyn Bridge. Early in its construction, Kingsley, on a motion proposed by Boss Tweed, was paid 15% of all construction costs. This was an unheard-of amount for such a large contract; when Tweed fell from power, Kingsley's payments were slashed. Notice the bronze plaque on Kingsley's monument. It explains that this large piece of granite was formerly a part of the bridge that united the Cities of New York and Brooklyn.

William C. Kingsley, the Brooklyn Bridge's contractor, as he was depicted on the front page of the July 5, 1873, edition of Frank Leslie's Illustrated Newspaper. *By 1873, the Tweed Ring had been forced from power, and those who had profited from its largess, including Kingsley, were fair game. Fowler, on the left, was a Commissioner of the Brooklyn Board of City Works; he was involved in yet another scandal with Kingsley involving the latter's work on the Hempstead Reservoir.*

Return to Battle Avenue and retrace your steps west to the first intersection, where it meets Hemlock Avenue. At the southwest corner of this intersection (to your left and across Hemlock Avenue as you proceed into the intersection) is the Howe family plot, circled by a low gray granite curb. Walk over to it. This is **STOP #33**.

William C. Kingsley's monument is made from granite that was once a part of the Brooklyn Bridge.

This advertising card was distributed by a salesman for Elias Howe's sewing machines.

Note the beautiful cut-leaf Japanese maple tree inside this plot, on the right as you face the plot. The central monument is marked "HOWE" across the front, and is topped by a green bronze bust of **Elias Howe** (1819–1867), who invented the sewing machine. Howe was a penniless Yankee mechanic whose invention sewed five times faster than the swiftest hand-sewer and made Howe a millionaire.

The bust is by Charles Calverley. Go into the plot and walk behind the bust; look up and you will see Calverley's signature at the bottom of the bust.

Now turn so that your back is to the bust and you are facing towards the back of the plot. Here is Fannie the dog's dark granite stone memorial. Take a few moments to read the impassioned verse across its front to this canine with the "limpid eyes."

Someone in the family of Elias Howe, the inventor of the sewing machine, felt strongly about their dog Fannie, erecting this monument, with its heartfelt verse, to the dog with the "limpid eyes."

Head back to the entrance to the Howe plot. As you leave, turn left and proceed west on Battle Avenue. Continue on Battle Avenue until you reach the first tomb on your left, which is about two-thirds of the way down the block. "DALY" is carved above the entrance. This is **STOP #34**.

In 1882, Irish immigrant **Marcus Daly** (1841–1900) headed to Montana, where he discovered one of the world's greatest concentrations of copper. Daly became the "Copper King," controlling every mine in Butte, Montana, and producing one-fourth of the world's copper. Butte's residents led the nation in per capita income, union membership, and suicides by dynamite. Daly personified the American dream; within 20 years of his arrival as a penniless immigrant, he was a multimillionaire owning mines, banks, power plants, irrigation systems, and vast tracts of timber.

Now turn, with your back to the Daly tomb, and walk across Battle Avenue to the Durant hillside mausoleum. This is **STOP #35**.

Thomas Durant (1820–1885) was the chief figure in the promotion, financing, and management of the Union Pacific Railroad, the great rail project which united America's east and west coasts. On May 10, 1869, Durant was given the honor of driving the Golden Spike to complete the Transcontinental Railroad.

Thomas C. Durant and other officials posed for this historic photograph upon the completion of the Transcontinental Railroad. Durant is the very tall man standing in the front row, just to the left of the tracks.

This is the largest of three sculptures by John Moffitt inside the Durant Mausoleum. Behind a locked iron gate and heavy granite door, they have been seen by only a few people in their more than one century of existence.

Continue to the west along Battle Avenue until you reach its intersection with Border Avenue, which comes in from the right. As you reach the middle of Border Avenue, look to your left; 18 feet off Battle Avenue is a granite stone with "McDONALD" across its front. Go over to it; this is **STOP #36**.

Take a minute to read the epitaph of **R.H. McDonald** (1820–1903), the '49er "who crossed the plains on pack mules" and was a "total abstainer" from liquor.

Continue on Battle Avenue a few feet to the nearby intersection with Fern Avenue.

If you're running short on time, you may want to follow Battle Avenue back down the hill to the main entrance; restart the walk here some other time. If you do head down Battle Avenue, watch for cars coming around the first curve.

Just across the road from the Durant Mausoleum is another unusual monument memorializing an individual's accomplishments. It describes the life of T.H. McDonald, '49er "who crossed the plains on pack mules," and lauds him as a "total abstainer" from liquor.

If you'd like to continue the tour, make a left onto Fern Avenue. After 100 feet, you'll reach the intersection with Mulberry Avenue. Just across Mulberry, at the southeast corner of the intersection with Fern, and just to the left of the Mulberry Avenue sign, is the eagle-topped marble monument to Colonel Abraham Vosburgh. This is **STOP #37**.

On April 22, 1861, as the Civil War began, Colonel **Abraham Vosburgh** (1825–1861) marched at the head of the 71st New York State National Guard as it hurried off to Washington, D.C., to protect the nation's capital from Confederate attack. Vosburgh was soon dead of consumption, and

Colonel Abraham Vosburgh barely had time to get his elaborate uniform dirty before succumbing to disease.

became one of the Union's first casualties. President Lincoln laid a wreath on Vosburgh's body as it was transported through Washington, D.C., and the colonel's unit erected this monument. Note its inscription, "Pro Patria" (For Country). This monument was originally surrounded by a cast iron fence, with the posts cast to look like bayoneted rifles. If you look carefully, you can see a low circle around the monument, worn down by the feet of thousands of 19th century visitors paying homage to the colonel. If you stood here on Decoration Day a century ago, you would have seen the veterans of the 71st Regiment firing three salutes to their fallen leader.

Marble, the white stone in the Vosburgh monument, is an excellent material for carving, but it does not weather well. Note the sugaring, the roughening of the surface, which is caused by a chemical reaction between the stone and acid rain. Compare this weathering to the granite at the base of this monument, which shows little, if any, wear.

The monument to Colonel Vosburgh, with its cast iron fence, circa 1870. Note that the posts of the fence were cast as bayoneted rifles. This was a very popular tourist attraction; a path was worn just outside the fence by the thousands who came to pay their respects.

A detail of the Pilot's Monument, showing its marble storm-tossed waves.

Return to Fern Avenue, face south, the direction you were going on it, and look off to your right, into the distance, for a wonderful view of New York Harbor and New Jersey in the distance. This is **STOP #38**.

You are walking across the glacial moraine, where approximately 17,000 years ago the glacier reached its southernmost point, then began to recede. Green-Wood's hills and ponds were formed by this glacier, and it left the rock debris which was raked off the cemetery's hillsides and was used to form its roads. Those small rocks are still visible today along the edges of Green-Wood's paved roads.

Also note the cherry trees to either side of the road. These mature trees are a pleasure in the spring, when they are in full bloom.

Now continue to walk south on Fern Avenue. On your left, about 180 feet from the intersection that you just left, rises a marble monument, topped by the figure of Hope supporting an anchor. This is the Pilot's Monument and is **STOP #39**.

On February 14, 1846, harbor pilot **Thomas Freeborn** was just trying to do his job, to guide the ship *John Minturn* into New York Harbor. But a storm was raging, and the ship ran aground near the New Jersey shore. Though rescuers flocked to the beach, Freeborn and many members of the crew could not be saved.

Freeborn's remains were initially interred at the Rutgers Street Burial Ground in Manhattan. Within months of his death, his fellow pilots had this monument erected and his remains brought here. Of marble, it features many images associated with their profession. Across the front of the sarcophagus, the *John Minturn* struggles against the waves which drove it aground. A ship's capstan, with anchor cable coiled around it, is above, and a marble mast rises, topped by the figure of Hope.

Continue along Fern Avenue; when you reach the first intersection, where Fern Avenue intersects Atlantic Avenue, stop and look to your left, to the northeast corner. This is **STOP #40**.

Entwined columns.

On this corner is an interesting collection of obelisks, capitals, and urns. Between the Palmer obelisk (the obelisk, an Egyptian form, harkened to an ancient civilization which had survived through many generations) and the Grant urn-topped column you will see two intertwined columns. These columns symbolize two young brothers, united in death as they were in life.

Though you will see several Victorian symbols in the cemetery, including many variations on the urn (symbolizing the body, which remains after resurrection has occurred) and the shroud (the fabric which covered the body and also remains on earth after the soul has arisen), throughout the cemetery, these intertwined columns are very unusual.

Now turn left at this intersection and walk down Atlantic Avenue approximately 200 feet to the first path on your left, Warrior Path; turn left onto it. Walk towards the classical male figure 100 feet ahead and to the right. This is **STOP #41**.

This is the monument to **Isaac Hull Brown** (1812–1880), the longtime sexton of Grace Church on Broadway in Manhattan, "the most fashionable and exclusive of our metropolitan Courts of Heaven."

Note the name at the base of the figure: "PYTHAGORAS." Why him? Was Sexton Brown fascinated with the hy-

Isaac Hull Brown's monument.

potenuse of a right triangle? Hardly. Sexton Brown was New York City's first social arbiter, a man with unparalleled knowledge of the most intimate information on every household in his parish. If you wanted to plan a fashionable party, Sexton Brown had all the necessary intelligence as to whom to invite and whom to snub. The good sexton knew more about his chosen subject than anyone else. And that's where Pythagoras came in. According to Pythagoras's teachings, knowledge was the key to salvation and divinity. Apparently Sexton Brown thought that, because he knew more dirt about New Yorkers than anyone else, his reincarnation, as explained by Pythagoras, was assured.

Retrace your steps along Warrior Path back to Atlantic Avenue. Continue across Atlantic Avenue to Hydrangea Path (directly opposite) and proceed down that path about 40 feet. When the path turns to the right, leave the path and continue straight ahead, as if the path continued in a straight line, another 55 feet. At that point, look to your right and you will see the white marble Griffith Monument. This is **STOP #42**.

This monument is perhaps the finest sculpture in Green-Wood Cemetery. It honors **Jane Griffith** (1816–1857), who was not famous, but certainly was much-loved by her husband Charles. A 19th century housewife, she is pictured here on the steps of her domestic preserve, accompanied by the family dog at the top of the stairs, bidding Charles goodbye as he heads off to work. They lived in a wisteria-covered brownstone at 109 West 13th Street in Manhattan; the Sixth Avenue horse-trolley waits for him at the right. It is the morning of August 4, 1857, and this is their last farewell. When Charles returned home from work that night, he found Jane dead, the victim of "heart disease."

Detail of the monument to Jane Griffith, a marble gem still in fine condition, shows off sculptor Patrizio Piatti's exquisite work.

This monument was carved by Patrizio Piatti, an Italian-trained sculptor who worked in Manhattan. Note Piatti's faint signature ("P. Piatti N.Y.") at the lower right of the central panel of the monument, on a line below the horse-trolley and just above "1827." Piatti went to the Griffiths' brownstone house to study its details and worked from a photograph of Jane Griffith. The carving originally had the details of her face on it; those have weathered away over the years. But, by and large, this monument is is fine condition. Look at the topography around you; the location of this monument, set down in a hollow and facing away from the prevailing storms coming off the harbor from the west, has made the remarkable preservation of this masterpiece possible.

Charles Griffith (1813–1882) visited this spot weekly for twenty-five years until he joined his beloved wife in the ground below.

Return to Hydrangea Path, which is just behind the Griffith monument, turn left on it, and follow it toward the next road, Fern Avenue. As you approach within 30 feet of Fern Avenue, look to your left. This is **STOP #43**.

Notice the angel above you, recording sinners and saints.

Turn left on Fern Avenue and proceed to the next intersection, where it meets Greenbough Avenue. On the left, the northwest corner, just before you reach the intersection, is the

elaborate marble Canda Monument. This is **STOP #44**. Walk up the stairs in front of it; Charlotte Canda's name is carved below the effigy of her.

In the mid-19th century, this was the most popular monument at Green-Wood Cemetery, and may have been the most visited cemetery monument in America. Every Sunday, crowds gathered around it to take in its beauty.

On February 3, 1845, **Charlotte Canda** (1828–1845), an educated young woman who spoke five languages, celebrated her seventeenth birthday with a party. When the party was over, she and her father drove one of her friends home in a raging storm. But when Charlotte's father got out of their carriage to accompany the friend to her door, the horses bolted down Waverly Place, careened around the turn onto Broadway, and Charlotte was thrown from the carriage, landing on her head. Her frantic parents, summoned to the scene, arrived just as she died.

The design for this monument, 17 feet high, 17 feet deep, with 17 rose buds for her 17 years, was modified by her father from a plan Charlotte had worked on for a memorial to her aunt. Charlotte's effigy appears in the niche; above her, the heavens wait to receive her soul.

As you stand directly in front of the steps to the Canda monument, facing it, look off to your right, 25 feet past the

Charlotte Canda's Monument, as it appeared in 1847, just after its completion. Note the monument at far right, in a separate plot surrounded by its own fence; it is that of her nobleman-fiancé, who committed suicide in the Canda's house a year after her tragic death.

kneeling winged angel. There is the monument to Charles Albert Jarett de la Marie. Walk over to it; this is **STOP #45**

He was Charlotte's fiance; a year after her death, he committed suicide in the Canda's house. Because of his suicide, he could not be buried in the Canda plot, which is ground consecrated by the Catholic Church. A French nobleman, his coat of arms appears on his gravestone.

CHARLOTTE CANDA.
Died suddenly
BY FALLING FROM A CARRIAGE
on the night of the 3d of February 1845
being the seventeenth anniversary of her birth-day

On a stone in front of the main monument, together with Charlotte's name and the date and cause of her death, was carved a poem that reflected the resurrectionist attitude of the time. Though, after more than a century and one-half of exposure to the elements, the inscription can no longer be read, this circa 1870 photograph preserves it.

Retrace your steps back along Fern Avenue, heading west. When you reach the first intersection, where Fern Avenue turns sharply to the right, follow it. The second set of stairs on your left, which is about 75 feet ahead, leads up to the Bennett Monument. This is **STOP #46**.

As you walk up the stairs to get a good look at this monument, note the large sheet of granite with two bronze handles set into it just in front of the stairs and with "BENNETT FAMILY VAULT" carved into it. These handles allow burly workers to lift the stone off for access, down another set of stairs, to the burial vault. The monument in front of you was described by one 19th century observer as "a life-sized female figure, kneeling on a cushion in an attitude of prayer, commending her child, which is held in suspense by an angelic figure, to the Almighty Giver." This piece is made from the finest Italian marble. Note its wonderful location; look west to take in the New York skyline.

Buried here is **James Gordon Bennett** (1795–1872), the founder of the *New York Herald*. Bennett started the *Herald* with a $500 investment as a one-man operation. Under his leadership, it grew into the most influential newspaper in America. The *Herald* gave birth to tabloid journalism; as

James Gordon Bennett, who built the New York Herald *into a national and international power.*

Bennett often said, "The newspaper's function is not to instruct but to startle."

Bennett's *Herald* was known for its fictitious news, sensational opinions, reckless personal attacks, and disrespectful tone. One observer remarked that no man of his time had done more "to blunt the moral sense of the people" than Bennett. Another observer claimed that reporters who obtain their stories by spying through keyholes had learned their investigative techniques from Bennett. Four times in his life Bennett was beaten with canes by men who took exception to the scandalous stories he had published about them; each morning-after, Bennett entertained his readers with a first-hand account of his drubbing.

Retrace your steps back along Fern Avenue to the first intersection, where Fern meets Highland Avenue. As you turn right onto Highland, you will see a set of low stairs in front of you; behind them is the massive dark granite stone memorializing Henry Draper. Walk over there. This is **STOP #47**.

This unusual monument, a pentagon, honors **Henry Draper** (1837–1882), who pioneered in astronomical photography, including photographs of the moon. His father, John Draper, also a scientist, was Samuel Morse's partner in their pioneering photographic experiments; both are buried at Green-Wood Cemetery. Carvings of several of the scientific awards Henry Draper received are on the back of his monument.

Note the dark granite sphere, marked "Auld," in front of and to the right of the Draper monument. This round stone is from a quarry in Quincy, Massachusetts, the only quarry in America which made this form.

Return to Highland Avenue, which runs in front of the Draper lot, and proceed left on it. On the left side of the road, what appears to be vacant land is in fact the unmarked graves of Mexican War veterans. This is noted on the map as **STOP #48**.

Continue along Highland Avenue a short distance until you reach the intersection with Atlantic Avenue. Here, on the northeast corner (in front of you and slightly to your right and across Atlantic) is one of the many monuments in the cemetery to firemen. It is **STOP #49**.

This early monument honors **Augustus LaFayette Cowdrey**, a young member of Engine Company #12 who died in the Great Explosion on Broad Street, July 19, 1845. Notice the fire-related imagery, the hose and the parade torch, adorning this monument.

Turn west onto the path that enters this intersection, Bay Side Path, and proceed down the hill about half-way; on your left, about 50 feet away, you will see the marble statue of a young boy. Walk over to it; it is **STOP #50**.

Frankie (Irwin Franklin), who lived from 1877 to 1880, is described as the "beloved son of Rear Admiral Aaron Ward," who is himself buried a few feet away. The figure is by famed sculptor Daniel Chester French, who is best remembered today for his statue of Abraham Lincoln at the Lincoln Memorial in Washington, D.C., and his Minute Man in Concord, Massachusetts.

The Egyptian Revival Johnston Mausoleum.

Just to the right of Frankie (as you stand in front of him and face him) is the Johnston mausoleum; walk over to it. It is **STOP #51**.

This is a good example of Egyptian Revival architecture, which was very popular in the 1830's and 1840's. Though critics of the time criticized this style as pagan and unchristian, and one critic even went so far as to describe it as "the architecture of cats and deified crocodiles," it was used widely in cemeteries and for prisons.

Note these characteristics of Egyptian Revival architecture: the battered sides (which angle inward as they proceed upward), the large overhanging cornice at the top, and the designs of the columns and capitals.

The layout here is unusual, with gravestones, including one for John Taylor Johnston, to the right and in front of the family's hillside mausoleum. More typically, individuals are interred inside such mausoleums and the names of the individuals interred are only visible inside that structure.

John Taylor Johnston (1820–1893) was the president of the New Jersey Central Railroad from 1848 to 1877. He introduced uniformed trainmen to this country, an idea which he brought back from England. Johnston also developed a private collection of paintings which had no equal in America. His collection included icons of American art such as Frederic E. Church's *Niagara*, now owned by the Corcoran Gallery in Washington, D.C., Turner's *Slave Ship*, currently in the collection of the Boston Museum of Fine Arts, and Winslow Homer's *Prisoners From the Front*, now at the Metropolitan Museum of Art. Johnston lived by a creed which he expressed early in life: "I consider it just as much my duty to give to benevolent institutions as to pay my butcher's bill." Playing a key role in the founding of The Metropolitan Museum of Art, he donated $10,000 to it, and in 1870 he was elected its first president. He was also president of the University of the City of New York, serving from 1872 to 1886. He endowed a Latin professorship there, gave the Law Library its start, and began the University's general endowment.

Now turn with your back to the Johnston Mausoleum; the large bronze statue of De Witt Clinton is directly in front of you. Walk over to it. It is **STOP #52**.

The City Hall Park unveiling of the Clinton statue, which was destined for Green-Wood, was the front page story in New York's Illustrated News *on June 4, 1853.*

When Green-Wood Cemetery was founded in 1838, the most admired man in New York was **De Witt Clinton** (1769–1828), who had died only a few years earlier. Read the description of his life on the base of the monument; this was one very busy public servant.

In its early years, Green-Wood Cemetery struggled to establish itself as a viable not-for-profit business. But receipts were lagging, and the survival of the entire enterprise was in doubt. Someone came up with an idea to drum up publicity and make the cemetery respectable in a single stroke: bring Clinton's remains to the cemetery. Green-Wood obtained permission from a Clinton descendant, had him disinterred

from Little Albany Cemetery, and he was brought to this spot. The public excitement was tremendous; prints were sold of the spot where he would be buried. This statue was paid for by public subscription and in 1853 was exhibited in City Hall Park in Manhattan before being brought to this spot.

Notice that the statue of De Witt Clinton is on a grass island. Head west a few feet towards the other end of this island; in the grove of evergreen hemlock trees you will find the monument to Nathaniel Currier. It is **STOP #53**.

This is the **Nathaniel Currier** (1813–1888) of Currier and Ives fame, printmakers to the American people. In all, they issued more than 7,000 lithographic prints from 1835 until the end of the century, and sold millions of copies of scenes of city and country, railroads, steamers, hunting, and other views. Currier's partner, James Ives, is buried about one-half mile away in another section of Green-Wood Cemetery.

Come down the stairs in front of the Currier plot and walk straight ahead. When you reach the first intersection, where Bay Side Avenue forks, follow the right fork. At the next intersection, where Bay Side Avenue meets Battle Avenue, turn left. As you do so, stop and notice the angel on the corner, to your left, above the Gerard Mausoleum. This is **STOP #54**.

James Gerard (1794–1874) was a public-spirited citizen who was very involved with public education in New York City. However, his greatest legacy is the uniformed police force. In the 1840's, when there were no uniformed police anywhere in America, Gerard traveled to England, where he admired uni-

Early New York City police uniforms.

formed bobbies, then launched a one-man campaign to have New York's "rattle watch" exchange its motley collection of rags for uniforms. Gerard had his tailor make up a costume of blue coat and buttons which he wore to a fashionable costume party. Soon New York's finest were in uniform.

This sculpture dresses up James Gerard's mausoleum.

Continue down Battle Avenue toward the main gates and the exit from the cemetery.

As you walk, notice the large trees along the left side of the road. These are Norway maples, trees which survive very well in an urban environment. They are pollution-tolerant and can be "limbed-up" (their lower limbs can be removed), allowing traffic to proceed close by them.

Thanks for visiting the cemetery. We hope you had a good time and you'll come back again for another visit.

Want to know more?

Also available from the Green-Wood Cemetery—

Brooklyn's Green-Wood Cemetery: New York's Buried Treasure.

"Fascinating"—*Maine Antique Digest*

"Lavishly Illustrated"—*Brooklyn Bridge Magazine*

"Dig In"—*Time Out New York*

⧗ ⧗ ⧗

This book, published by the historic Green-Wood Cemetery and printed by Stinehour Press, one of the top printers in America, is for everyone who enjoys a good story about New York, its people, and their legacy. Lavishly illustrated, with 90 color and 379 black and white images, it features the great visual delights of Green-Wood Cemetery as well as some of the outstanding art created by the people who reside there.

Green-Wood Cemetery has its share of the famous (Leonard Bernstein, Samuel F.B. Morse, Peter Cooper, Horace Greeley, Louis Comfort Tiffany, Henry Ward Beecher, General Henry Halleck, Lola Montez, Laura Keene, Elias Howe, and Frank Morgan, to name a few) and the infamous ("Boss" Tweed, Albert Anastasia, Joey Gallo, and Johnny Torrio). Here's your chance to enjoy their stories and tales of spiritualism, psychics, resurrection, the Civil War, the tragedies of the *Arctic*, the *General Slocum*, and the *Morro Castle*, infant death, the early years of baseball, the history of New York and Brooklyn, and much more.

Author/photographer Jeffrey I. Richman is an attorney in New York City. He has been haunting the cemetery for years, researching and writing its story.

☞ Order this book from the Green-Wood Cemetery by mail at 500 25th Street, Brooklyn, N.Y. 11232, or by phone at 718 768-7300. It is $50, and shipping is $3.